MW00627358

The Plant-Life Chronicles of a Seattle Gardener

TIM CLEMEN

Text and images ©2018 by Tim Clemen

Second printing

Cover: *Hibiscus syriacus*, rose of Sharon

Book design by André Mora
Typefaces: Atlantik, Fern, Rhody

Printed in the United States
by Edition One Books

to Phyllis Hatfield
Thank you for being my writing coach and friend!

Contents

Preface

I'VE BEEN A LANDSCAPER since I jumped into the pool at the townhouse complex down the street from my parents' house at midnight with my buddy Rick, yelling, "Sonics are number one!" It was 1979, and the Seattle SuperSonics had just won the NBA Championship. I was bouncing on the diving board when Mr. Tipp, the president of the Woodcreek Homeowners' Association, threatened to have us arrested for trespassing.

He pulled out a pad and paper and took notes as he interrogated us.

"Boys, I want your names, addresses, and phone numbers—and no funny business."

We could have run, but we were good boys. We gave him the information.

"And how old are you?"

"Fifteen," we answered sheepishly.

"I'll give you kids two choices," said Mr. Tipp.

"Your parents can pick you up at the Bellevue Police Department tonight, or you can show up ready to work tomorrow morning at seven thirty sharp."

Rick and I got there early that Saturday, and Mr. Tipp put us to work weeding the common areas until he brought us sandwiches at lunchtime. At the end of the day, he gave us another two choices: "I can pay you now for an excellent day's work, or you boys can start your summer jobs on Monday."

When I graduated from Bishop Blanchet High School three years later, I had real job experience. After that, I dabbled in college, commercial fishing, and travel for many years, but the binding theme was always landscaping—in Seattle, London, Berlin, and Vienna. It wasn't until my midthirties that I finished my degree in philosophy from Seattle University, between Bering Sea crab and Bristol Bay salmon seasons. More than a decade on the ocean had left me wanting to keep my feet firmly planted on the land, so I started my own landscaping company. It's been a hard row to hoe, but nowadays Tim's Gardening, LLC stewards some of the finest estate gardens in Seattle.

Thirty-eight years now, and I've worked in hundreds of gardens. And while I worked I swapped stories woven around plants with clients and coworkers, because the garden is a place for storytelling, and plants are living archetypes that we infuse with narrative. Guaranteed, if you are a person who is fortunate enough to have your own garden, and we do a walk-through together, you will tell me some plant stories—that hardy fuchsia was from your best friend's garden, or this weeping willow reminds you of summers at the swimming hole down at the arboretum. As for me, every manner of tree or shrub that I've ever planted, pruned, or simply beheld, I associate with a place and a person, and these are some of my stories.

The Walnut Drops Close to the Trunk

Juglans pershiana
ENGLISH WALNUT

My father was a business manager at Boeing, but his father was a farmer in Ipswich, South Dakota, a forgotten railroad town that the family fled due to abject poverty. It was 1942 when they left. Dad must have been twelve at the time. Grandpa and Grandma packed up seventeen of their eighteen children and headed out west to Seattle. I imagine them travelling in a convoy of overburdened pickups, like in a Steinbeck novel.

Uncle Louis, Dad's oldest brother, who could shoot the eye out of a skunk from two hundred yards out with his .22 rifle, was grown by then and stayed behind. Some months later, Grandpa had to go back to bury him in the Holy Cross Cemetery there in Ipswich, after the Model T Ford he and his buddies were hot-rodding in got hit by a freight train.

Dad had a bunch of stories about growing up on the farm, like the time he and his brothers stole strawberries "as big as your fist" from a neighbor's place. He got the strap for that one. Or the time Grandpa Henry rescued him from up top the outhouse by grabbing the escaped bull by the nose ring. And he told us about the old shade tree that grew near the house—an English walnut.

Dad used to climb out the second-story window and shimmy down the trunk of that *Juglans regia* like a monkey in order to beat his brothers to the warm kitchen where Grandma cooked porridge on the woodstove. He said they slept three to a bed and shared shoes, too, but my siblings and I never believed him. Just like we doubted that the boys had one set of coveralls each, and no other clothing except their hand-me-down coats. We didn't know anything about bitter winters on the prairie or walking for miles to school through snow because we grew up soft in Bellevue. I always loved hearing his stories, though, and for as long as I can remember, I dreamed of having my own piece of land with an English walnut on it.

He was nearing the end of his days when Lulu and I bought our place out in Bremerton. I tried to get him over to see our five-acre spread with a creek winding through it, but he was too weak by then. Two English walnuts grow side by side near the entrance like sentries. He would have been proud to see them there so far from Ipswich and his youth. He was just a little guy when the family left, standing in front of the black-and-white farmhouse surrounded by dust and siblings, captured forever in a photo.

A Pocket Full of Conkers

Aesculus hippocastanum
HORSE CHESTNUT

I REMEMBER ONE SUNDAY after church at the Immaculate Conception on Capitol Hill being knee-high in bluebells searching for horse chestnuts under my grandmother's massive *Aesculus hippocastanum*. When my mother informed me that the horse chestnut tree was older than Grandma, I was shocked. I didn't know that trees could live so long.

"It's a wise tree that keeps its secrets," said Mom. "That's what my brother said when he climbed down from the top of that thing after he came back from the War in the Pacific. He stayed up there for hours. I could hear him talking to it."

The furrowed trunk branched out into young leaves and candelabra blossoms that were white with dashes of pink and yellow at their centers, invigorating the atmosphere with their aroma.

"Can you eat the nuts? I asked.

"No," said my mother, "they're poisonous. The squirrels won't even eat them." She is descended from a long line of German farmers. The love of plants is in her blood. "Notice how each leaf has seven leaflets. That's how you can tell that it's a true horse chestnut rather than the red horse chestnut which only has five leaflets per leaf."

I arranged the polished nuts, known as conkers, into spiraling circles on the dried leaves beneath the tree until Mom went back up into the kitchen with Grandma. My siblings were playing Red Light, Green Light with some cousins on the lower lawn, and Dad was pacing near the horse chestnut, unawares, as I snuck up the hoary tree like a monkey. I climbed higher than I had ever climbed before. I could see pigeons perched on the dome of Grandma's church across the street. That dome was painted like the Sistine Chapel inside—or so it seemed to me when I was eight— cave drawings compared to the glory of the horse chestnut I was hugging.

My father muttered to himself as he paced, taking an occasional drag on his cigarette or stopping to light another. He had recently taken a pay cut at Boeing, but he still worried about losing his accounting job there after the extensive layoffs in 1970 Seattle. That morning, when we were on the way to SeaTac (Seattle-Tacoma International Airport) to pick up my aunt, Sister Betty, in the station wagon, we saw a black-and-white billboard that read, "Will the Last Person Leaving SEAT-TLE—Turn Out the Lights."

"You be careful up there," Dad said, surprising me. "You're a good fifteen feet up." I waved to my mom through the kitchen window. Grandma was pointing at something. I could see my mom's lips moving, but the window was painted shut. Just then the rotten branch I was on cracked under my weight and I tumbled toward the earth.

Before I could hit the ground, though, Dad caught me. My old man had some "guns" on him back in the day, decades before the pancreatic cancer whittled him down to a stick figure of his former self. "I told you to be careful," he said, as tears sprung from my eyes. I tucked my face under his arm and listened to the sound of his heart thumping faster than mine as he carried me to the car, my pockets full of conkers. "Get the kids, Charlie," he said to Mom, using his pet name for her. "It's time to go home."

Stogies Under the Smoke Tree

Cotinus coggygria
SMOKE TREE

WHEN I WAS TWELVE and the leaves would fall, I'd rake them up and bag them for our neighbors, Margie and Ray Mueller. They had a row of Lombardy poplars along the property line like a farmer's windbreak. I'd get two bits a bag for gathering their golden bounty. The money I made, though, was always secondary to the dream of diving into a billowy leaf-pile like I had seen somewhere in a children's book. Sadly, every leap ended in a splat because western Washington was a soggy place in autumn.

When I was done raking for the day, Margie would be waiting by the sliding glass door with a glass of Shasta cola for me. As Ella and Louis bickered about diction over the hi-fi, Ray would pay me in cash. One time I made over three dollars, and Ray said, "You sure are a conscientious young worker."

Before the Muellers started their surveying company, Ray cruised timber for lumber companies in Colorado, Washington, and Oregon. He had weather-beaten skin, sapphire eyes, a bad hip that caused him to limp, and an unlit cigar clenched between his teeth. Ray was always there with blunt pragmatism when I needed someone to talk to other than my dad. When a neighbor boy was bullying me, I went to Ray. He sat me down under the shadow of a small tree bursting with blossoms.

"Stop crying, Timmy," he said, "and take a look at this here smoke tree. It's my favorite plant in the garden." I wiped my eyes with the inside of my T-shirt, wondering where he was going with this. "They call this the *Cotinus coggygria*. That means 'tough as nails' in Latin."

"It looks like pink smoke," I said.

"Those are panicles—clusters of tiny flowers." Ray's voice had a gravelly authority and he knew his trees. "I planted that thing in hardpan a decade ago and haven't watered it since, and look at it."

Sitting there in the shade of the *Cotinus coggygria* something unusual happened. Ray lit his cigar. "I know that boy, Jimmy; he's a bully." He took a drag off his stogie, held it introspectively, and exhaled a blue cloud that intermingled with the blossoms of the smoke tree. "The only thing a bully understands is this," Ray said, raising a wizened fist.

The next day, while riding my bike through the neighborhood, I happened to pass Jimmy's house. Leaning back on my sissy bar, I rolled by, slowing and casting him the evil eye, and Jimmy threw a rock at me. Ditching my bike in the middle of the cul-de-sac, I charged at him like an angry bull. He didn't even have time to run when I swung—with no consequences, except that his mom called my mom and my mom said, "What would you like my Timmy to do, just let your son throw rocks at him?"

I checked in on that smoke tree the other day, when we were all gathered at my mother's place for Thanksgiving dinner, 2017. I was surprised to find that it was still alive and looking as handsome as ever, but it didn't seem to have grown much since I was twelve. I lit the cigar that I had been saving. Lack of nutrients, I thought, and forty-two thirsty summers. But it outlived old Ray Mueller, and it will outlive me, too, because the *Cotinus coggygria* is one tough tree.

The Tree of Life

Fagus sylvatica (Purpurea Group)
PURPLE LEAF BEECH

IN SEATTLE'S VOLUNTEER PARK, just south of the Conservatory and north of the Asian Art Museum, lives a purple leaf beech tree whose grey trunk is ten feet across and scarred with the initials of long-ago lovers. It has been growing there since the Olmsted Brothers redesigned the park a hundred and ten years ago. Countless hippies have hung out in those branches. The last time I went out on those limbs was the summer of 1982, the night of my first Grateful Dead concert.

The Lower Queen Anne neighborhood that sides the Seattle Center venue was crowded with VW vans plastered with Deadhead stickers that looked like they'd been following the band since the sixties. I was there with two prep school buddies, Tim W. and B. Malloy—freshly graduated from Blanchet High School and eager for adventure.

Inside the Coliseum a long-haired dude said, "For the genuine experience you need to find the guys wearing purple tie-dye. You'll see them standing near the columns." They were selling tiny pieces of blotter paper portraying dancing bears for three bucks a hit. Clueless Catholic boys at a Dead concert, we took the sacrament and boogied with the flower children.

Jerry Garcia was singing "Mama Tried" when everything turned to Technicolor: the purple and green radiances illuminating the stage, the spotlights slashing through the colorful crowd, and the blue notes of the rhythm section that made me dance like a heathen. When the show was over and the hippies went back to their vans, we began an odyssey that brought us to one of the oldest purple leaf beech trees in the city.

Passing through the Seattle Center that was built for the 1962 World's Fair, we drank deep from a spigot that Tim W. found in one of the gardens, then ran fully clothed through the International Fountain that someone had neglected to shut off for the night. We walked through the labyrinth of hushed carnival rides and under the looming Space Needle. Ambling onto Denny Way, we passed the neon Elephant Carwash sign.

"If I was king of this concrete jungle," Tim W. said, "I'd demolish everything and plant a forest."

"I'd keep my city," I said, "but plant a massive tree on the corner of Sixth and Battery where I could just sit and think."

"Not me," said Malloy. "I'd trade it all for a 7-Eleven. A large Slurpee would really hit the spot right now."

We passed the Lincoln "Toe Truck," with gigantic pink toes jutting up from the cab, and crossed under an I-5 viaduct to the western slope of Capitol Hill. After summiting the Howe Street Stairs, we found ourselves on the grounds of St. Mark's Cathedral, observing the ebb and flow of lights on the freeway. I marveled at a lone seagull.

"Where's a shotgun when you need one," said Malloy.

We entered Volunteer Park just before dawn and found that purple leaf beech tree. *Fagus sylvatica*, the tag read. We were reclining on its Rubenesque limbs when red dawn erupted over the Cascade Mountains, igniting the canopy like burning bronze.

"Good God!" I gasped.

"Jesus H. Christ," said Tim W. "This is the tree of life."

Malloy just stretched out on his limb like it was a poolside lounge and said, "Life's a beech and then you die."

No Sanctuary

Liriodendron tulipifera
TULIP TREE

I KNEW THE Parcheesi game had gotten out of hand when one of the Cuban refugees I was playing with nearly drove a butcher knife through my chest. Maybe I shouldn't have taken the victory lap around the table with my hands held high, chanting "Cubans suck at Parcheesi," but since I had managed to beat a kitchen full of Cuban ex-cons three times in a row at their favorite game, I couldn't help gloating.

It was a hot summer night in Portland, Oregon, and I was barefoot and eighteen. My Spanish wasn't too good back then, but I knew enough to know that I couldn't let Roque say those things about my mother, so I shoved him to the floor. "We're taking this outside," I said, oblivious to his proximity to the knife block. I was putting my shoes on as he spanned the dirty geometry of the linoleum floor and lunged at me with the butcher knife—the big one that Father Chuck was always sharpening.

As I threw myself backwards, everything seemed to move in slow-mo—the hovering flies, the scattering Cubans, and the glimmering steel arcing toward my heart. But when my back hit the beer-soaked floor, the knife came up short. Roque was raising the blade for a second assault when I rolled to my feet and took off screaming through the rectory, knocking over furniture to hinder his pursuit. I needed to stand and fight and I knew it, but found nothing strong enough to strike him with.

I reached the front door, but there was no time to open it because that hound of hell was on my heels. I dashed through the dusty chapel, through the long dining room, and back into the kitchen, which was clear except for Armando—before whom I stood breathless and disgraced. When Roque came in, the blood-rage was gone, and his eyes were mere pits of despair. I probably should have cracked him with the chrome-and-vinyl kitchen chair, but I couldn't. Armando said something to him in Spanish, and they left.

I walked out to Dawson Park across the street and sat on the sod with my back against the towering tulip tree, the *Liriodendron tulipifera*, wondering what I had gotten myself into. Except for the white noise of the freeway, silence reigned. I wanted life experience, but not like this.

I had made a one-year commitment to the

Immaculate Heart Catholic Church in Northeast Portland, assisting in the elementary school and food bank. Up to that point, things were going pretty well. I had become part of the church's community, and Sunday mornings found me singing with the gospel choir—"You've got to wade in the water, wade in the water, children, because God's going to trouble the water."

When my dad dropped me off five months earlier, he studied the scarred faces of the Cuban refugees that Father Chuck, the parish priest, was sponsoring, and told me to be careful. By nightfall, I was laughing and drinking with my new housemates, Francisco and Armando, as if we were old cellmates. When the malt liquor ran out, Armando busted out the chapel wine and we played Parcheesi into the night.

"They call us Marielitos," Francisco said, as he described bloodying his arms on the barnacle-encrusted hull of a capsized skiff amidst rumors of sharks, prior to the US Coast Guard rescuing him off the coast of Florida—a refugee from the Mariel Boatlift. It had been in the news a few years before. President Carter told Castro that the US would accept political prisoners, but Castro pulled a fast one and sent a bunch of hardened criminals along with them.

The lawn around the tulip tree was dotted with yellow petals that seemed to glow under the sodium-vapor streetlight. Sitting there with my back against the five-foot wide *Liriodendron tulip-*

ifera, I felt safe. A warmth seemed to emanate from the trunk. Picking up a fallen branchlet, I gazed at the tulip-like flower, yellow-green with orange at the center. How can something so small propagate such a colossus, I thought, looking upward into the eighty-foot canopy. That's when I noticed a figure approaching through the gloom.

"What's up, blood?" rasped Francisco. "Armando told me about what happened. Timmy, you got big trouble now. Roque killed three guys in detention camp in Miami, and more back in Cuba. You're going to have to get him before he gets you."

Early the next morning, I went for a run, past the corner store where I had recently broken up a knife fight, past the Dawson Park bathroom where a homeless man had died from alcohol-induced hypothermia, past the stately tulip tree, and over the dark girders of the Burnside Bridge crossing the wide Willamette River swirling to the sea.

Father Chuck was in the kitchen when I got back. I told him about my close call the night before, but he didn't seem to get it—as if epic events only happen in ancient books where oceans turn to blood and water turns to wine. Now that I think about it, he should have called the cops or at least given me some spiritual advice. But I didn't need a priest to tell me that *Thou Shalt Not Kill* is a good commandment. I learned that from my parents.

I called my father, but he was busy watching a game and passed the phone to my mother. "Come home, Timmy," she said—but I didn't. I had committed to one year there and was determined to see it through. After what happened with Roque, though, I was always looking over my shoulder.

Weeks before my volunteer commitment at Immaculate Heart Church ended, Armando told me that Roque had crashed his Mercury Cougar on Interstate 5 and had died. I went for a walk that ended in Dawson Park, with me sitting against that grand specimen of a tulip tree. Bowing my head in prayer, I said some encouraging words for Roque's tortured soul, then raised my eyes to the soaring *Liriodendron tulipifera* and laughed out loud.

Garden Guru Ciscoe

Corylus maxima 'Purpurea'
PURPLE FILBERT

MY BIG SISTER, Annette, helped me get a work-study job at Seattle University on the summer landscaping crew with Ciscoe Morris. It was 1983 and he was still in charge of the vast landscape there, and not yet a household name. In a matter of minutes my interview was over, and we were talking about Goldie, his Labrador retriever, who went with him everywhere, even to President Sullivan's office near the corner of Broadway and Madison. Nestled beneath that busy corner of Capitol Hill there was a garden, Ciscoe's garden, featuring a grouping of purple filberts—plants so sublime that each season's color display surpasses the last.

In summer, the broad ovate leaves of the *Corylus maxima* 'Purpurea' are a burgundy color with tinges of green. In the fall, they turn a brilliant yellow with ripe hazelnuts as highlights. Amethyst catkins adorn the stems through the cold months, until the mauve buds of spring begin the cycle all over again.

I wish I could say that those purple filberts were the first plants that Ciscoe ever taught me to prune, but no such luck. The first pruning lesson he gave me was on a spray of *Cotoneaster horizontalis* (rock cotoneaster, a deciduous shrub) growing over a basalt rock wall. Ciscoe taught me to prune out the dead wood and thickest growth so that the branches and leaves cascaded over the boulders like jade-green water. As he moved on to help the next crew member, he said, "Don't be afraid to really go for it. If you make a mistake, just remember, it's a plant. It will grow back."

I'll never forget those summer days when we'd all pile into the back of the pickup trucks and head down to Madison Park for lunch on the lawn by Lake Washington. We'd circle around Ciscoe to listen to his stories, like when he got his nickname dressing up as The Cisco Kid for Halloween in Wisconsin, or about the exotic gardens he'd visited and people he'd known in Europe and Japan.

Once after lunch, he treated us to a pruning demonstration on his filberts. The crew watched in silence as he sized up the first one like a Zen master. Drawing his Swiss-made Felco hand pruners like a gunslinger, he cut several branches in quick succession, slipped the pruners back in the holster, and said, "Voila!" I couldn't believe it; he had improved upon perfection.

When I left Seattle University to start my first gardening company, Ciscoe was always there with advice on business and design. He knew all facets of the industry, and when he moved on to become the Pacific Northwest's gardening guru on radio and television, I wasn't surprised. Sometimes people get what they deserve.

I saw him walking with his wife, Mary, a few years back, while I was pruning a purple filbert over in the Sand Point neighborhood. We shook hands, chatted for a bit—he asked how my sister was, and I thanked him for inspiring me to pursue my life's work.

Loss in the Blossoms

Blossoms

LAYERS OF LEAD PAINT were peeling off the dilapidated duplex that Dave and I had just rented in Bellingham, but we didn't care. Nor did we mind (because the rent was cheap) that the two-story building was leaning visibly. There was a partial view of Bellingham Bay, and Western Washington University was just three blocks away.

I had already registered for the 1984 fall quarter and would be taking Art History, Northwest Native Plant Identification, and Russian Literature. Dave was taking business classes. "Boring," I said. "I hate business."

"I get it, man, you're artsy-fartsy. But like it or not, business is in everything we do, including the arts."

"Right now, I'm in the business of just living," I said.

Priscilla, the Air-force brat living upstairs, hated business, too. She was studying graphic arts, had been all over the world, could play Tchaikovsky on her flute, and was supercute. When we met, she was wearing cutoff jeans, an evil eye necklace, and a tie-dyed T-shirt that read, *Join the Marines, travel to exotic places, meet new people, then kill them.*

The first time I was alone with her, Priscilla showed me the pink silk tree, flowering defiantly amidst the blackberries and bindweed growing below our domicile. "That's what sold me on this place," she said, "the pink silk tree. We had one in our courtyard in Izmir, Turkey, where my dad was stationed when I was a girl. He was a colonel." The convoluted branches held delicate leaves with pink blossoms that looked like diminutive pom-poms. It reminded me of something from a Doctor Seuss book. "It's in the pea family," said Priscilla.

"That's Fabaceae," I replied, and we kissed under the bipinnate leaves.

Priscilla and I became inseparable. "Attached at the hip," Dave used to say. We studied together, hiked and dirt-biked in the Chuckanut Mountains together, and drank a lot of coffee at Tony's Coffee House over in Fairhaven. I'll never forget how sweet it was when we got snowed in for a week after the students had all gone home for break.

The old boiler in the basement only heated her place, so we stayed up there, occasionally venturing out onto the snowdrifted streets to buy bread and wine, then back to our refuge overlooking the frost-covered branches of our leafless silk tree. When the blizzard cleared and the streets were plowed, Priscilla's mother came up to drag her back to Seattle for Christmas but didn't invite me. That woman never took a liking to me.

We were still together the following spring when the leaves reappeared on our *Albizia julibrissin* 'Rosea,' but by August we had broken up—or more accurately, she had broken up with me. As if to put a wreath on our coffin, they demolished our love nest, and tore that pink silk tree out by its roots before it could even blossom. To this day, every time I see one in full bloom I think of Priscilla, because they can destroy the tree, but they can't erase the memory.

The Overhand Right

Forsythia × intermedia
BORDER FORSYTHIA

THERE WAS A *Forsythia × intermedia* in the vacant lot by the Hillman City Boxing Gym, whose yellow flowers punched through the drab of winter like fists of sunlight. The gym was in the Rainier Valley where the real estate was cheap in the mid-eighties, and the shops all had bars on the windows. The rhythm of punches resounded through the old warehouse as I filled out the waiver that Bob Jarvis, the ex-pro fighter who owned the place, left on a card table. *I voluntarily assume all risk of injury, accident, and death*, the form read.

Jarvis was talking to an old man who held a cane in his fist like a conductor with a bludgeon while training a big guy on a heavy bag. I was signing on the bottom line when they called me over. "This here is Joe Toro Sr., the Godfather of

Seattle boxing," said Jarvis. "He's going to have a look at you."

I hit the heavy bag while the two of them took turns barking orders at me: left jab, right hand, uppercut, left hook. I did the best I could. "The kid's got no jab, no left hook," complained Joe Toro in his gravelly baritone. "But I like that big right hand of his." Toro reminded me of a Puerto Rican version of the old trainer in *Rocky*, but tougher.

"You've been playing around with that karate, haven't you, kid?" said Jarvis. It was true, I told him, I had trained at a dojo for a while. Jarvis rolled his eyes, "You'll never get any power out of your punches if you don't get your feet right."

"Don't worry about it! I'm going to break him of that habit," said Joe, "Now, get started shadowboxing in front of the mirror. You're with me now." I couldn't believe it. I felt like I had just won a thousand bucks on a scratch ticket, which was funny, because I just went in there on a whim. I wanted to try something new after a hard day of landscaping.

"That's right, Johnny!" Joe shouted to the boxer he was training. "Now finish it off with that overhand right I been teaching you." Johnny took a hop back and delivered an arcing fist that buckled the heavy bag like a sledge hit it. "Good night, Irene!" said the Godfather of Seattle boxing.

I was pretty tired when I left that first day, but I broke off a couple of border forsythia stems for my girlfriend just as Joe Toro was shuffling out.

"Nice flowers," he said. "I grabbed a piece of that when I was back in Jersey visiting my family last week."

"*Forsythia intermedia*, the border forsythia," I said.

"Sounds like you know a little something about plants."

I told him that I worked for the best landscaping company in Washington State—R. David Adams, Inc., putting in gardens that cost millions of dollars, and that an Englishman named Robert Aspinall was mentoring me. "He's the best landscaper in Seattle," I said.

"I stuck that stem in the dirt out in my front yard," said Joe. "Do you think it will live? It was my mother's."

"It might make it if the soil is good and you keep it watered all summer," I told him.

After a week of training, Joe put me in the ring with Johnny, his heavyweight, saying, "You're just gonna spar. Half-speed. I want you to get the feel of the thing." By the first bell I was exhausted and bleeding from the nose. Joe pulled a cotton ball from his pocket and said, "Shove this up in your nostril and get back in there."

Toward the end of the third round I heard him say, "All right, Johnny, show me that overhand right," and the big man dropped the hammer, followed by a left hook that emptied my lungs, leaving only pain where the air had been. Somehow, though, I was able to sneak in a right hand to the heart followed by a left hook to the head.

When the bell rang, Joe said, "You boys want to keep fighting?"

Before I had a chance to quit, Johnny spoke up. "I'm done."

I staggered down from the ring looking for a water fountain and was washing blood from my face when Joe tottered over. "You better watch that water," he cautioned. "Drink too much of that and your muscles will cramp up." He was always saying old-school stuff like that. "Now let me have a look at that nose."

"I think it's broken."

Joe just laughed, "Don't worry about it! You look better that way." I asked him about my ribs. "Cracked or bruised," he said. "The doctors can't do anything about them, anyway. Same with the nose. I'll keep you out of the ring for a couple weeks and you'll be as good as new."

I was surprised to see that Johnny was absent the next day. "What happened in there," I asked Joe. "I thought we were just supposed to be sparring?"

"You read the waiver," he growled. "You should know that when you're in the ring, you're facing death. Don't be so hard on yourself, kid. You did pretty good for your first time."

I drove him home to his Ballard double-wide that night, where Joe kissed his wife indifferently and said, "This here is Timmy, one of my fighters. He's going to stay for coffee, but first we're going to take a look at that forsythia I brought back from Jersey."

Blanche had silver hair and pink cheeks, and her dress matched her apron. "That poor thing," she said. "I don't know how you think it will ever live."

"Just make us some coffee," said Joe, "and bring us some of that lemon meringue pie I bought at the Safeway."

Lodged in hardpan with two of its four leaves wilting, the *Forsythia × intermedia* cutting looked like a lost cause. Joe sat on a folding chair in the middle of the weed-infested lawn watching me till the soil around the sprig, which I had dipped in rooting hormone. I mixed fertile mulch and fertilizer into the nutrient-poor soil, and then gave it a long drink from the watering can to which I had added a few drops of Superthrive. "I love to watch you work," said Joe.

At the gym, I doubled down on my efforts so that I would be ready the next time I had to spar. Joe taught me to alternate my feet while skipping rope and to tap a rhythm on the speed bag, only resting when the bell rang. I'd do sit-ups off the side of the ring while he bounced the medicine ball off my gut, and when I worked on the heavy bag, he'd say, "Snap those punches like you're cracking a whip." I remember the night he taught me the overhand right. I felt like I had drunk from the Holy Grail.

I started driving Joe home after my workout

every day, making sure that the border forsythia start stayed watered. Sometimes I'd take him up to the Veterans Hospital on Queen Ann Hill for his cataracts, high blood pressure, diabetes, or heart problems. I told him that the only thing keeping him alive was that he was too mean to die.

"You got that right, Timmy," said Joe, limping on both legs.

Almost a year had gone by when it struck me that Joe Toro Sr., the Godfather of Seattle boxing, who had run the old Eagles Gym in downtown Seattle for over twenty years—training and promoting local legends like Boone Kirkman, Ibar Arrington, and Mike Lankaster—was training me to be a professional fighter. But the truth was, my heart wasn't really into it. The learning curve was too painful, and I wasn't hungry enough.

Before spring came again, I was ready for a change. I told Joe that I had decided to take a trip to Europe, but he didn't miss a beat. "You should drop by some of those gyms in London and Ireland that I used to take my fighters to," he said. "They've got some tough kids over there, but don't worry. You've learned from the best."

The day I drove over to say my goodbyes to Joe and Blanche, the *Forsythia × intermedia* was so laden with yellow flowers that I could see it from a block away. It had sprouted a half dozen canes, the longest of which was almost three feet tall. "You're in the right profession," said Joe. "That forsythia is a real knockout."

Big Clyde

Aesculus × carnea
RED HORSE CHESTNUT

I LANDED IN LONDON alone in early spring when white blossoms were just appearing on the almond trees in front of the youth hostel near Holland Park. I was lured to the hostel by an Australian woman handing out flyers at the Charing Cross Railway Station. "For every five guests, I get a week's free rent," said the tall blonde with a wink. "I'll be seeing you back at the guesthouse, then?"

I was twenty-two and had enough money for a couple of frugal months backpacking across the Continent. I figured I'd be in London for a week at best, but there is a sprawling gravity to that city that doesn't let go of the traveler easily. I saw the sights, visited the great museums and gardens, and hit the pubs with people from all over the world, but I didn't meet any English people until I ran out of money.

It was a Saturday morning when it dawned on me. I was sitting in the back garden of the hostel contemplating the sixty-two-foot red horse chestnut heavy with viridescent panicles. A cup of coffee and my money belt sat on the rusty table before me vying for my attention. When she wasn't peddling beds at the train station, Natalie ran a little café in the hostel's common area selling Nescafé and biscuits. "*Aesculus carnea*," I said, as she brought by another coffee, "the red horse chestnut. You can tell it from the standard horse chestnut because there are only five leaflets per leaf."

"Horticultural names are hot," she said, moving on to the group of South Africans chatting with some Gambians under the tree. I examined the contents of my money pouch. There was my American passport with only one stamp in it, a return ticket to Seattle, and enough English pounds to last a week. *No problem*, I thought, *I just have to get a job.*

I walked the building-boom streets, going from one construction site to another, until I found two Irish brothers whose three-piece suits were covered in dust—demolition men. Their brogues were cryptic, but I grasped that they paid in cash and needed someone who was handy with a sledge hammer. "I'm your man," I declared.

The work involved gutting old council houses slated for retrofitting in the central London borough of Earl's Court—removing century-old lath-and-plaster walls and molded ceilings, and collapsing three-story chimneys in dust-spewing avalanches. At times the air was so thick that my teeth would be black when I took off my dust mask.

I worked with a couple of Irish guys living in the East End. They'd invite me on their pub crawl some Sundays to watch Celtic folk-punk bands jam Pogues-style while we tossed back pints of Guinness. We were up at their flat one night eating blood pudding and chips when they started talking about the Brixton riots of 1981. The neighbors were dropping bricks on the bobbies from the fourth floor, they said.

The only Englishman I worked with was a Cockney who was always trying to incite me—somewhere it is written that there must be one like him in every workplace. I never laid a fist on him, though; I just outworked him. When he got fired, he said that I was a geezer and that he'd gotten himself a bottle of steroids on the black market, and he'd be back to kick my "arse" when he got buffed.

I got my friend on as his replacement. Big Clyde, a Kiwi from the hostel, was loud and liked to fight. His favorite sport was rugby, which he played in an amateur league back in New Zealand. "No pads, mate, not like your poofter American football." Clyde came to London to escape a shotgun wedding. "I'm not much fond of being on the business end of a scattergun," he said, "but that's not why I left. I left because I'll be goddamned if

I'll let a woman blackmail me with an unborn baby."

Clyde was a demon with a sledgehammer, and together the sum of our labor was greater than twice what either of us could accomplish alone. Before we knew it, the governors were giving us our own jobsites. With smudged faces and ragged clothes, we'd ride home on the old bicycles we had purchased at Camden Town Market and drink beer under the burgeoning red horse chestnut tree with our hostel mates—refugees from the British colonies.

Clyde had a crush on an Austrian student named Katerina, who spoke five languages and had eyes that were bluer than the Danube. It strained our relationship when I slept with her. We were working in a half-demolished edifice the day I told him I was sorry. "It was her choice," I explained, "how could I say no?"

Gripping his double-bitted axe in both hands, Clyde did not look happy. Without warning, he sent the axe flying like a lopsided boomerang until it connected with a plate glass window, shattering it into hazardous fragments. "It's all right," he said, as he sauntered over the crunching glass to retrieve his twibil. "I reckon I'd do the same if the tables were turned. It just makes me think that I don't belong here."

The last time I saw Big Clyde, the red horse chestnut was in full blossom, filling the hostel with the scent of clover honey. "I'm going back home," he said. "It's time for me to be a father to my son."

"You'll be a good dad," I gasped, as he bear-hugged the air out of me.

The Guest
Workers

Tilia cordata
LITTLE-LEAF LIME

THE LIMESTONE STEPS of our third-story flat
in Vienna were depressed from the generations
of tenants who had trudged upon them. The place
overlooked the Danube Canal, had a sink, a sin-
gle-burner stove, and a bathroom down the hall
which we shared with the whole floor. A couple
of months after Big Clyde went back to New Zealand, Katerina and I had used the last of our
money to move there from London.

Our first day in town, we went to the University of Vienna, where she spoke to some profes-
sors and secured enough tutoring gigs to last her
through the summer. Katerina was a linguistic
wunderkind—five languages—and her English was
better than mine.

The following morning, we started out on foot
looking for landscapers, but wherever Katerina
enquired, a work visa, which I did not have, was

required. My dependence upon her made me wish that I had applied myself more in high school German. We wandered until we found ourselves on the outskirts of the city where a hillock covered in scrub revealed crumbling ramparts and a *Tilia cordata* that was older than Napoleon. "There sure are a lot of these little-leaf lime trees here," I said, admiring the brawny specimen, heavy with lime-yellow blossoms and honey bees.

"In German we call them *Lindenbaum*," said Katerina. "They're native to Europe." We followed the pathway down and around until we discovered that what we had taken for a hill was actually the remnants of an ancient castle with a cave where the gate must have been. "Let's explore," said Katerina.

Before I could object, she disappeared into a tunnel that opened into a dank cavern illuminated by greenish light. In the distance, figures labored in a mist. The mushroom farmers paused as we approached. The eldest pressed his wooden pitchfork into a pile of steaming compost, cap in hand, as Katerina addressed him. Luckily, he didn't need another laborer.

Back out in the sunlight, I said, "Jesus, woman, do you really want me to work in a frigging dungeon?"

"It's manual labor," she said with a laugh. "That's want you wanted."

We walked to the nearest phone booth where Katerina made a dozen cold calls before she found a landscaping company willing to interview me. "Yugoslavian guest workers," she said. "It's better than nothing." A couple of *Strassenbahn* (streetcar) transfers later, we arrived at the office just as the crew was coming in. Katerina translated while the boss quizzed me on my experience.

There were no formalities to mark my hire, except for a slap on the back from a grinning giant, and a shot from the vodka bottle being passed around. "The big guy is Lala," someone said in English. "His name means 'tulip' in Croatian. I'm Nebojsa, but you can call me Nesh."

"What's your name mean?" I asked.

"In Serbian, it means 'brave one.'" I asked him how he had come to speak English so fluently. "I learned from watching American sitcoms," he said. "I like *Taxi* and *Cheers* very much."

When I tossed back my second shot, they applauded—first time drinking with an American, I guessed. Nesh introduced me to the rest of the guys: Croats, Serbs, and a Slovenian basketball player who was the boss's nephew. But Katerina just wanted to get out of there. Walking back to the streetcar, I was on top of the world until she said, "I don't associate with them. They're dirty."

The next morning, I found myself at the wheel of a flatbed Mercedes, tearing down the Autobahn with a truck full of gardeners. "It's more than thirteen hundred years old," Nesh called out over the rushing air as we passed a crumbling monument. "The Austrians are so proud of it, but our churches in Belgrade are much better preserved. And they think we don't have culture!"

"Well, to be fair," I said, "they have a whole museum devoted to Gustav Klimt, the Mystical Symbolist."

"I love that museum," said Nesh.

That day was spent trimming a massive topiary hedge of little-leaf limes at a walled estate whose baroque gardens were reminiscent of the grounds at Schoenbrunn Palace. The closely sheared *Tilia cordatas* were over five meters tall. From a distance they looked like a boxwood hedge writ large. At lunch we drank beer beside a freshly raked pile of the heart-shaped leaves. Nesh said it was normal to knock back a couple of brewskis at lunch, but Lala and the boys had six each, and it was the strong stuff. "To Tito," said Nesh, raising his bottle, and everyone chimed in unpersuasively.

"Who's Tito?" I said.

"He was the president of Yugoslavia until his tragic death in 1980. You must have heard about it on the news in your country," said Nesh. "Tito was the greatest Serbian of his generation. He led the partisans to defeat the Nazis, and he stopped Russia when they tried to invade us. It's a tribute to his greatness that Yugoslavia is still united as one."

Lala cleared his throat. "Tito was born in Kumrovec," he said. "He was Croatian."

"Maybe," said Nesh, "but his heart was with us."

Dining with Katerina that night, she asked me how I liked working with the "Yugos."

"They're not bad for a bunch of commies," I joked, but she didn't laugh. "Actually, I like them a lot. They treat me well."

"You can't trust them," she said.

"Darling, don't you know us blue-collar boys stick together? Lala says we're part of the international proletariat."

"That's from *The Communist Manifesto*," said Katerina. "Karl Marx."

"It was required reading at my high school," I said, "and I take issue with you calling them dirty. I can personally guarantee that they're clean. They took showers and changed their clothes before leaving work today. And they warned me not to take the Strassenbahn in my dirty work clothes. Unlike you! Your people were pointing and laughing at me the whole way home."

"I'm sorry," said Katerina. "This is completely outside of my experience."

As the days turned into weeks, we quarreled more, and Katerina began coming home later and less often. I read all of her Kafka, Goethe, and Stephen King; frequented the Gustav Klimt Museum and the grand parks; or simply wandered the streets of the elaborate metropolis alone. I started hanging out more and more with Nesh and the boys. "You'd like Nesh," I said to Katerina. "I was thinking about inviting him and Lala over for dinner." She wasn't keen on the whole thing but went along with it, not saying more than a few words the whole evening and chain-smoking. Pretty antisocial for a person who aspires to do simultaneous translation for the United Nations, I thought. But on those nights when she let down her long hair and fell asleep listening to my heart beat, it all made perfect sense.

Then operations screeched to a halt at the end of July, and the boss informed the crew that he was shutting the company down for all of August. "Vacation!" Nesh exclaimed in delight. "I'm going back to Belgrade. My family will leave on holiday soon to the Adriatic. Would you like to come with us?"

That's when the thought grabbed me like an undertow—I hadn't seen my family and friends for almost a year. "Thanks, buddy, but I think I'm going home. It sucks to be broke in Vienna, and anyway this place is way too snobbish for my taste. I miss Seattle, where the gardens are glorious and the people are mellow."

"What about Katerina?"

"I'll invite her to come with me," I said. "The atmosphere there would do her good."

After the Fall
of the Berlin
Wall

Ginkgo biloba
MAIDENHAIR TREE

"ALL THE BIG GINKGOS in Berlin were destroyed during the war," said Alex. "You won't find one older than thirty years in the whole city." Alex had long hair, but he wasn't a hippie; he was a certified German landscaper of the first degree. He rolled up the sleeve of his green coveralls to show me the *Ginkgo biloba* leaf tattooed on his forearm, an ancient sign for hope and healing, he said.

Our boss was a landscape architect who regretted the destruction of the Berlin Wall. "It didn't keep us in," said Herr Schmidt, "it kept everyone else out. Artists, pacifists, musicians, and gays, like myself, flocked to West Berlin. They gave us an annual stipend just to live here, and we didn't have to do military service like the rest of Germany." He went on to point out that not only had the Wall provided the world's largest canvas for graffiti art, it was a reference point for drivers. Berliners never got lost; they just followed the Wall back to where they started. "Berlin was an island," said the boss, "our island."

It was 1990, a year after the Wall came down, but in many ways it was still there. I remember the first time Alex drove us past Checkpoint Charlie into the East Berlin neighborhood called Mitte. It was like watching the color fade from the world. The architecture droned on in charcoal grey and coal-smoke brown. "This place cries out for ginkgos," said Alex. "They make excellent street trees."

Alex was the only West Berliner with the company. He was worldly for someone who had grown up in a walled city. He worked a lot harder than the East Germans on the crew did. Herr Schmidt called them his "Zonis," slang for people from the zone outside the Wall. There was a former East German wall guard on the crew named Hans who Herr Schmidt called the "Stasi," but not to his face. The boss asked me if I knew how the wall guards had gotten promoted. "By shooting someone who tried to escape," he said. "Hans was a captain."

The boss called me the "Ami," short for American. I wasn't sure if that was good or bad, probably a remnant of the Cold War. Herr Schmidt and I communicated in a mixture of German and English. "Gerglish," he called it. Alex and the

Zonis didn't speak English at all, so I had to immerse myself in German. Within a couple of months, I could hack my way through almost any conversation.

Alex and I were the special projects team: laying paving-stone patios, pruning, and planting an array of florae, including maidenhair trees (*Ginkgo bilobas*), across the city. "Herr Schmidt and I try to include one at every job site," said Alex, "as living tributes to the unification of Germany." They were thought to be extinct, he explained, existing only as fossil records until an eighteenth-century botanist named Engelbert Kaempfer discovered ancient specimens growing in a Japanese monastery. Turns out that Buddhist monks had been cultivating ginkgos in China and Japan for eons.

East Berlin, West Berlin, we worked everywhere from Schoneberg to Prenzlauer Berg, but my favorite neighborhood was Kreuzberg, where I lived in a preschool whose owner rented me the space after the children had all gone home for the day. It had a kitchen, a couple of bathrooms, and naptime mats on which I slept when I wasn't out clubbing with friends until dawn, because Berlin's nightlife was legendary.

Getting paid under the table in Germany was a little dodgy back in the day. On one occasion, I was asked to show my papers by a resident of the apartment building where we were installing drainage. "Germany is for Germans," said the old man. "Americans can come to learn about our superior culture, but then you have to leave."

"Unfortunately, there are too many of those people still alive," said Herr Schmidt, while driving me to another jobsite where Hans was the crew chief.

Working with the Zonis was like watching ice melt, and Hans kept saying, "Slow down, John Wayne. You work like you're trying to conquer the frontier." It was a crisp fall morning when Alex brought me to a Charlottenburg courtyard to finish up a stone patio. The heavy lifting was a relief compared to the slow pace that Hans enforced until a couple of dudes in uniforms showed up. "One of those old-timers must have heard your accent," Alex said, coming to my rescue. "I'll meet you by the ginkgo trees at the Universitat der Kuenste."

I waited by the row of maidenhair trees, watching their autumn leaves flutter to the lawn like yellow butterflies. "It's not good," said Alex, popping the tops off the two Hefeweizen beers he had brought us. "The boss says he hates to lose his Ami but he has no choice. I thought you should hear it from me first."

"That's OK," I said, "I was getting kind of homesick anyway."

"The whole thing is disheartening," said Alex. "Just last year, I helped demolish the Berlin Wall with my own sledgehammer because I wanted to make Germany a more open place."

"We have the same problem in my country," I said.

"Then you must carry on our tradition. When you get back to Seattle, plant ginkgo trees."

The Motion in Her Potion Moved My Ocean

Hibiscus syriacus
Rose of Sharon

Puerto Vallarta was liquid pleasure, so I called for another Bloody Mary while my buddy danced to Regatón rhythms with some local girls on the lighted dance floor. Months of seventy-hour workweeks had landscaped the way for that Fourth of July trip, but I didn't feel like dancing. I just sat at the bar slurping the spice from my empty Mary while the alcohol flowed through my blood like love.

Beneath the music there was a deeper beat of waves crashing against the seawall outside the Malecón, where bronze sculptures by Mexican masters stand like watchtowers before the sea. Along the bar were hibiscus flowers, pink with magenta centers, in whiskey glasses. I asked the willowy beauty in a faded sundress two seats over from me how to say hibiscus in Spanish. "*Obelisco*," she said, looking like a model marooned there after a photo shoot.

"Are you Spanish?"

"I'm Mexican," she said, and as she said it, the sea breeze fraternized with her fragrance. "From San Jose del Valle, Nayarit, about an hour from here."

"I'm Tim. I'm a gardener from Seattle. It's a pleasure to make your acquaintance."

"Your Spanish is pretty good for a tourist. My name is Maria De Lourdes Amaral-Plata. The nickname they give you for all that here is 'Lulu.'" She motioned toward Rick, dirty dancing with one of her companions under the disco strobe. "Are you with him?"

"I've known Rick since we were kids. He's all right."

"The woman he's doing that with is Tina, my son's aunt. I'm not like that."

"Work hard, play hard," said Rick, ambling back to the bar with Tina under his arm.

"It's been nice meeting you," said Lulu, "but we have to go now. My one-year-old son is with the sitter, and it's getting late." She frowned at Tina. "You're still driving me home, aren't you?"

The next morning, Rick and I walked the winding path to the beach through the hotel gardens, bursting with tropical hibiscuses in reds, whites, and pinks.

"Happy Fourth of July!" said Rick. We were floating on our backs in the blue Pacific. Overhead, pelicans drifted through the troposphere. I didn't respond. I was thinking about my father's words after my divorce.

"When you meet someone you want to run off with again, imagine her as the mother of your children, and you'll know in your heart if you're doing the right thing." I told him that I didn't want to have children. "That doesn't matter," Dad said. "It's a metaphor."

A fish jumped. "Oh, by the way, I talked to Tina this morning." Rick was speaking. "We've got a lunch date today, and she's bringing Lulu."

By that afternoon, we were relaxing in leather chairs on the sand, eating ceviche and sipping micheladas. Rick pawed and Tina posed, both oblivious to the way in which Lulu swept back her windblown hair, gazing past the horizon. "You look beautiful," I said, staggered by the vision.

"I borrowed this dress from my sister. Tina told me we were going for a job interview."

After lunch, we piled into Tina's old VW and sputtered inland over the heat-mirage highway, passing grassy dunes and a rainforest. And then we were on a road filled with potholes. Tina's "Bug" stopped with a gasp before a stucco house. Barefoot children were playing in the dirt under an old mango tree. "This is the house I grew up in," Lulu said. "And that's my son, Luis." She sprung from the car, lifted him in her arms, and kissed him. "He needs a bath," she laughed, wiping his face with the back of her palm. "So we'll see each other tomorrow, then?"

WE ATE IN OLD VALLARTA, sipping red wine beside the moonshine sea. "When do you go back to Seattle?" she asked.

"The day after tomorrow. I was hoping we could see each other again before I leave."

Night gulls chanted to the pulsing surf. "I can't," she said. "My sister is having a birthday party for her son with piñatas, a cake, and a band playing ranchera music. We've spent days preparing for it. By Monday we'll all be so broke that we'll be eating tortillas and beans until our next paychecks—with no regrets." She raised her glass, as trumpet blasting mariachis traipsed onto the terrace.

We went to the disco, but we didn't dance. We just sat in a corner booth with a black-light conquistador hanging over our heads. Lulu spoke first: "I don't feel comfortable here. People will get the wrong idea." Just then, an old man snapped a Polaroid of us. "I need to pick up my son now."

She allowed me to share my taxi, driving down lanes where only the locals go, until Lulu told the cabby to stop beside a yellow tenement. Vanishing into the shadows, she returned with Luis slumped over her delicate shoulder. "We're staying the night at my sister's," she said. "It's not far from here."

This is it, I thought, as we pulled away from the curb. *If I don't do something, I'll never see her again.* So I sang Lulu the only love song I knew, "Buckets of Rain," by Bob Dylan—about the way her motions move me, the way her smile reaches me, and the cool way her eyes see right into me. I sang it in English, so she may not have understood a word of it. But when the car stopped again, she asked me in.

There was a note on the table beside a tarnished pewter vase chock-full with the freshly cut hibiscus. "It's from my sister," she said, laying Luis upon the couch. "She'll be home soon. Can I get you a glass of water?"

And suddenly we kissed under the clattering fan.

I COURTED HER by commercial airlines, commuting a couple times a month until we tied the knot. We rented a house next door to her sister's place, and after many months of navigating an expensive immigration process overburdened with paperwork, we started anew in Bremerton, just a ferry crossing away from Seattle, where my landscaping company is based. The place needed some work, but we made it a home.

One spring day, we planted a *Hibiscus syriacus*, the rose of Sharon, outside our bedroom window. It's the hardy cousin of the tropical hibiscus common in Puerto Vallarta—pink with a magenta center—like the ones at the bar that night on the Malecón, when we met on Independence Day.

The Titian Pith
of Alders

Alnus rubra
RED ALDER

FEBRUARY 1, 2010

Slogging up that mountain in four inches of late snow was like running in wet sand. My feet were drenched but warm in my Vibram FiveFingers shoes; it felt like I was running barefoot. My cell phone rang—another bill collector. I slipped on the icy summit amidst a stand of red alder trees, landing flat on my back as the ringing stopped.

As I lay there waiting for the pain to subside, I gazed at the *Alnus rubras*. Their lichen-painted trunks shone white like a grove of European birches in the golden hour. Strange, I thought, that a handsome tree like the red alder is considered a weed here where it grows best, while we fill our gardens with plants that aren't even native to the Pacific Northwest. When it was almost dark, I pushed myself up, knocked the snow off my ass, and kept running, because it's winter in the Great Recession.

FEBRUARY 6, 2010

I was lucky enough to have a full day of pruning in Broadmoor today. I've made my business doing garden renovation, but Seattleites have stopped spending. Before the recession, that gated neighborhood was bumper-to-bumper with contractors, but today mine was the only service vehicle in sight. The first to go were the landscapers. If you ask me, economists should track our industry like a canary in a coal mine to predict economic disaster.

FEBRUARY 12, 2010

I run in the evening with the dogs after the kids are fed and read to, and the dishes are done. It's important to bring a headlamp because the game trails and abandoned logging roads are hard to find in the dark. My wife, Lulu, worries about me because there are bears up there, but a long run in the hills eases the stress so I can sleep.

This evening, I stopped where the power lines crest the hill before descending into our valley to watch night fall in waves around a solitary red alder that was mauve with ruddy catkins. Under the *Alnus rubra* were the tracks of two startled deer. The snow they kicked up was evidence of their haste.

Tracking them through the snow-crushed ferns, I spied a doe with her fawn motionless in the draw until Angel, our border collie mutt, broke from heel and they were gone. Tobi Blue, our Bouvier des Flanders, held his ground, though, looking up as if to ask, What now, boss?

FEBRUARY 22, 2010
We awoke to the rumble of rain battering our metal roof last night, and water dripping onto the bed. "What next?" I moaned. "We can't afford a new roof! I'll be amazed if we can even keep the house."

"Don't worry, baby," said Lulu, "this is nothing." And she spread a painting tarp over our duvet. "When I was a little girl in Mexico during hurricane season and the roof would leak, my father would climb up there and put a piece of chewing gum in the hole." And with that I slept like a child in her slender arms.

MARCH 5, 2010
There is something primeval about running with your dogs far from home, knowing there's a strong likelihood of getting lost. My cell phone rang, then stopped. I was out of range, thinking about something my father used to say: "I should have been born a hundred years ago; I would have been a mountain man."

MARCH 20, 2010

I ran the Mercer Island Half Marathon today with Tim W. It was transforming. There was a shared passion among the throng more profound even than running with my dogs. I thanked Tim, saying that I never would have gotten back into running if it hadn't been for him.

After the race, I went to work in the Montlake neighborhood, pruning a garden for a surgeon whose husband had won his age group that day. He acted as if my accomplishment were nothing, but for me it was everything.

APRIL 15, 2010

The days are getting longer, and my days are filled with work all over the city in gardens that have been neglected—and I'm ready. I jogged down a deer path tonight, through sprays of trillium blossoms bordering a red alder grove. *Alnus rubra*—I repeated the name like a mantra; it flows off the tongue like poetry, an underdog tree with the qualities of a champion.

Rounding a bend, I spotted a three-hundred-pound black bear grazing on a patch of horsetails not ten yards ahead. I stopped in my tracks, found a sturdy stick, and began battering the trunk of an alder and shouting at the top of my lungs until the bear bolted into the salmon berries. "Worthless mutts," I muttered. "You didn't even notice it was there!" The titian pith of the red alder looked like rusted blood where I broke the bark. That must be where it gets its name from, I thought, as Tobi Blue brushed up against me, wagging his stubby tail.

MAY 20, 2010

I did my first marathon today, 26.2 miles around Eugene, Oregon, ending at Hayward Field, where Steve Prefontaine ran his last race. Tim W. drove me there but couldn't run due to a torn hamstring. He rode his bicycle instead, supporting me with gel packs and water every five miles and cheering me on. But for the last 6.2 miles, I was on my own and cramping up. It took everything I had to collapse across the finish line in four hours and twenty minutes. "I knew you could do it, buddy," said Tim, "because you don't quit."

"Running a marathon is just like real life." I said. "The secret is to just keep your feet moving."

References

If you'd like to know more about the trees and shrubs featured in this book, I recommend using Missouri Botanical Garden's online Plant Finder. Or, for the real plant nerds, check out the *Manual of Woody Landscape Plants* by Michael A. Dirr. It has everything!

Acknowledgements

Thanks to the multitalented André Mora, for designing this book. And thanks to my editor, John Eckard—you rock. Thanks to photographer Lara Gale for taking the headshot of me.

To Lulu, my life-partner, thanks for the time and love you invested in reading and discussing my manuscript.

To Luis, my son, thanks for the *Forsythia × intermedia* pictures. And to my son Diego, for the *Alnus rubra* and *Juglans regia* pictures.

And a singular shout-out goes out to author Dennis P. Eichhorn, best known for his autobiographical comic books: *Real Stuff* 1 and 2, and *Extra Good Stuff*. You read everything I ever wrote, my friend, except for this one. Sorry you aren't alive to see it.

About the Author

Tim Clemen owns and operates Tim's Gardening, LLC in the greater Seattle area. He was born in Seattle and has lived in Europe and Mexico, visited a mouthful of other countries, and speaks Spanish fluently, but his German has gone completely rusty. Tim spent over ten years fishing commercially in Alaska for salmon, herring, and Bering Sea crab. Presently, he and his wife, Lulu Clemen, live with their two teenage sons, Luis Guerrero and Diego Sebastian, on their acreage bordering the wilderness outside Bremerton, Washington.